D1417313

THINGS ARE ALIKE

and DIFFERENT

By Illa Podendorf

Illustrations by John Hawkinson

CHILDRENS PRESS, CHICAGO

Illa Podendorf, former chairman of the Science Department of the Laboratory Schools, University of Chicago, has prepared this series of books with emphasis on the processes of science. The content is selected from the main branches of science—biology, physics, and chemistry—but the thrust is on the process skills which are essential in scientific work. Some of the processes emphasized are observing, classifying, communicating, measuring, inferring, and predicting. The treatment is intellectually stimulating which makes it occupy an active part in a child's thinking. This is important in all general education of children.

This book, *Things Are Alike and Different,* emphasizes the classifying process. Characteristics such as shape, size, and color are identified, and single-stage, double-stage, and multi-stage classifications are made.

Copyright © 1970 by Regensteiner Publishing Enterprises, Inc.
All rights reserved.   Published simultaneously in Canada.
Printed in the United States of America

Library of Congress Catalog Card Number: 79-123801

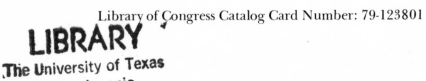
LIBRARY
The University of Texas
At San Antonio

5 6 7 8 9 10 11 12 13 14 15 16 17 18 19 20 21 22 23 24 25 R 75 74

CONTENTS

Almost Alike......................4

Find the Likenesses.................8

Find the Differences...............11

Using Likenesses and Differences....12

Flowers Are Alike and Different......17

Leaves Are Alike and Different.......24

Animals Are Alike and Different......36

ALMOST ALIKE

You can see how these blocks are alike.

They all look like the same shape.

They all are cubes.

They all have red, blue, and black on them. But one is different.

You can see how these balls
are alike.

They all look about the same
size and the same shape.

They all are spheres.

They all have the same colors
on them. But one is different.

You can see how these boxes are
alike. They are rectangular.
    They are almost alike in other ways.
How are they different?

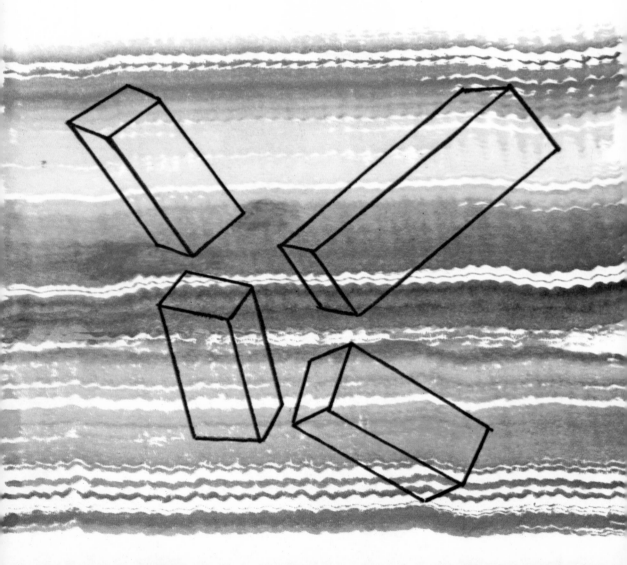

You can see how these cans
are alike. They are the same size.
They are the same shape. They
are cylinders. It is easy to see
the curved parts of cylinders.
One can is different. Can you find it?

FIND THE LIKENESSES

Here are different shapes.
They have different colors.
Can you see a way in which
they are alike?

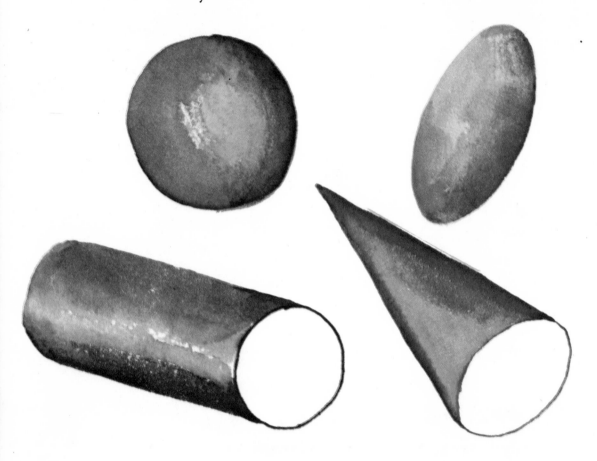

They all are curved in places.

John found some things that were
alike in one way.

It was the same thing that made
the shapes on page 8 alike in one way.

These things look very different
from each other.

They have different shapes.

Some have one color, and others
have more than one.

How are they alike?

You might say that they all have
straight sides, or that they all
have points.

FIND THE DIFFERENCES

These things are the same color.
They are about the same size.
Can you see how they are not alike?

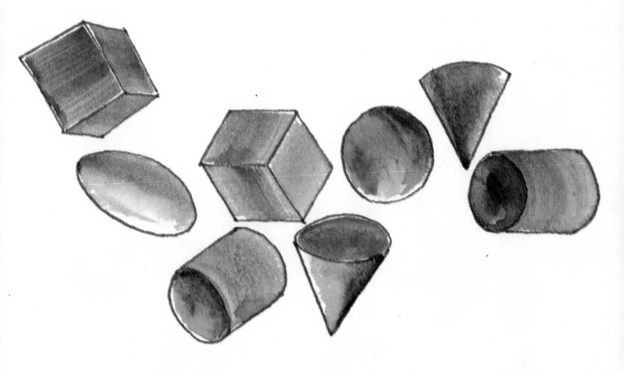

Did you see that it is only
the shapes that are different?

USING LIKENESSES AND DIFFERENCES

It is the characteristics of things
that make them alike or different.
Color, shape, and size are some
characteristics. We learn to look
for characteristics of things.

John used characteristics when he made two groups of the objects like those on page 12. Can you see which characteristics he used?

WITH CURVES

WITH NO CURVES

John used the shape of the things.
Shape is a good characteristic to use.
It could be done in other ways, too.
These things are grouped in another way.

MORE THAN ONE COLOR   **ONE COLOR**

Can you find a way to put all
the things with straight sides
and points into two groups?

Color is a good characteristic
to use when making groups.

RED

NOT RED

16

FLOWERS ARE ALIKE
AND DIFFERENT

These flowers are all
the same kind. Some are
different in one way.

Can you use this difference
and put them into two groups?

The next page shows you a way to do it.

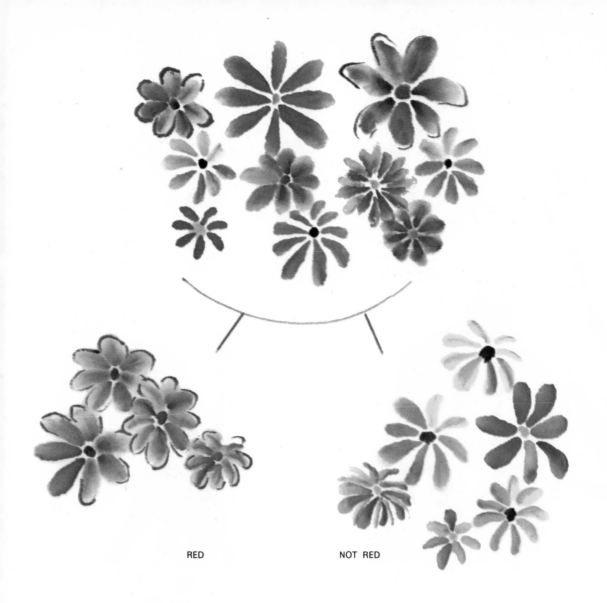

RED

NOT RED

Can you make two groups of the flowers
that are not white?

Would your groupings look like those
on this page?

Or perhaps your groupings look like this.

Here are more flowers. They are all the same color.

Can you find a way to put them into two groups?

It is easy to find a way if you notice the shapes and sizes.

Look on the next page.

All these flowers are the same in two
ways. But they are different in another.
Can you use this characteristic to
put them into two groups?
What characteristic can you use?

Is the characteristic size?

LEAVES ARE ALIKE AND DIFFERENT

Here are pictures of six different kinds of leaves. Each leaf has a name.

Each leaf looks different than the others.

Can you see what the differences are? They are alike in some ways, too. Can you see how they are alike?

DOGWOOD

ELM

MULBERRY

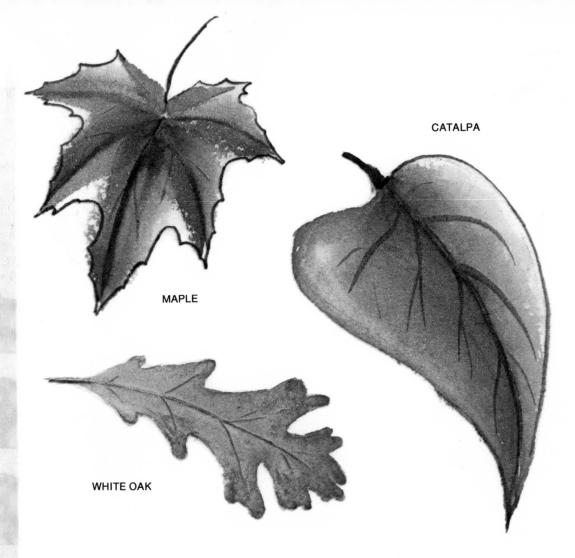

CATALPA

MAPLE

WHITE OAK

Did you notice the color? It is the same.
Did you notice the shapes? They are different.
Did you notice the edges? They are different.
Did you notice the lengths? They are different.
Did you notice other things?

Jimmie made two groups
of the leaves.
Here is one group.

Here is the other group.
Can you see his reason for grouping
them as he did? Look on the next page.

Some leaves were
longer than his ruler.
Some leaves were
shorter than his ruler.

Alice grouped the leaves in a different way.

She put all those on this page in one group.

Can you see her reason for doing it as she did?

Look on the next page for a hint.

Did you notice that Alice used the
leaves that did not have smooth edges?
These on this page do have smooth edges.

Mary made two groups of the leaves.
Can you decide which characteristics
she used?

Look on the next page for a hint.

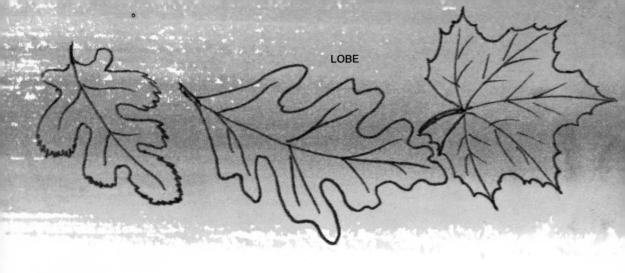

LOBE

Some leaves have lobes.
All the leaves above have lobes.

Some leaves do not have lobes.
These leaves do not have lobes.

Then Mary divided all the lobed leaves
into two groups.

Can you see how she did it?

Did you notice the points on some of
the lobes?

Mary divided all the leaves without lobes into two groups.

She did this the way Jimmie did it on page 28.

Jimmie, Alice, and Mary have been doing a special thing.

They have been making a chart.

They said they *classified* the leaves.

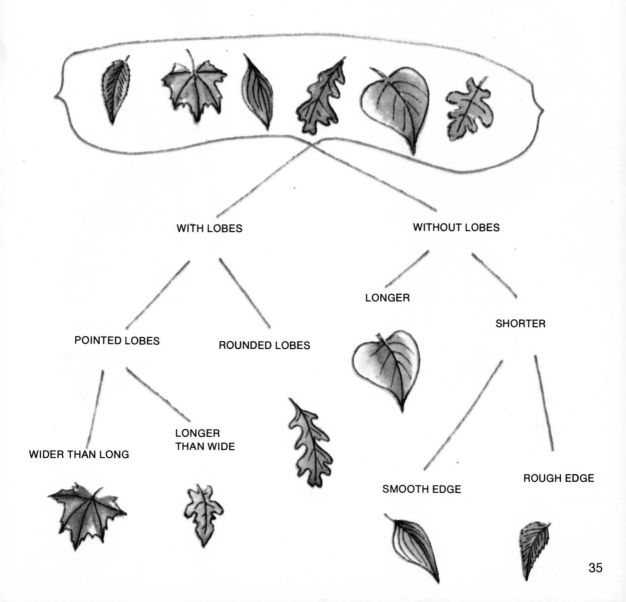

WITH LOBES

WITHOUT LOBES

POINTED LOBES

ROUNDED LOBES

LONGER

SHORTER

WIDER THAN LONG

LONGER THAN WIDE

SMOOTH EDGE

ROUGH EDGE

ANIMALS ARE ALIKE AND DIFFERENT

Animals can be classified, too.

There are many characteristics which can be used. Here we will use only characteristics that can be seen.

We might use two feet or four feet.
We might use tail or no tail.
We might use ears that are longer than the tail or shorter than the tail.

Look at the two groups of animals
on these pages. Give each group a name.

Does your name
have the word "wings"
in it?
You could say,
"Animals with wings."

You could say, "Animals with no wings."

Here are two more pages of animals.
Can you suggest a way to group them?
Think of a name for each group.

Does the name have
the word "leg" in it?

Here is a chart of a classification
of animals. This classification is
based on characteristics that can be seen.
Can you give each group a name?

Were your names the same as these?

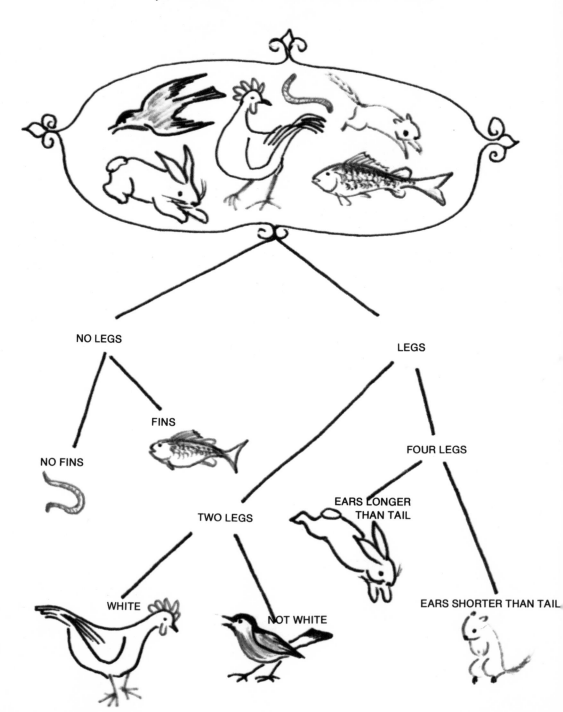

NO LEGS

LEGS

NO FINS

FINS

FOUR LEGS

TWO LEGS

EARS LONGER THAN TAIL

WHITE

NOT WHITE

EARS SHORTER THAN TAIL

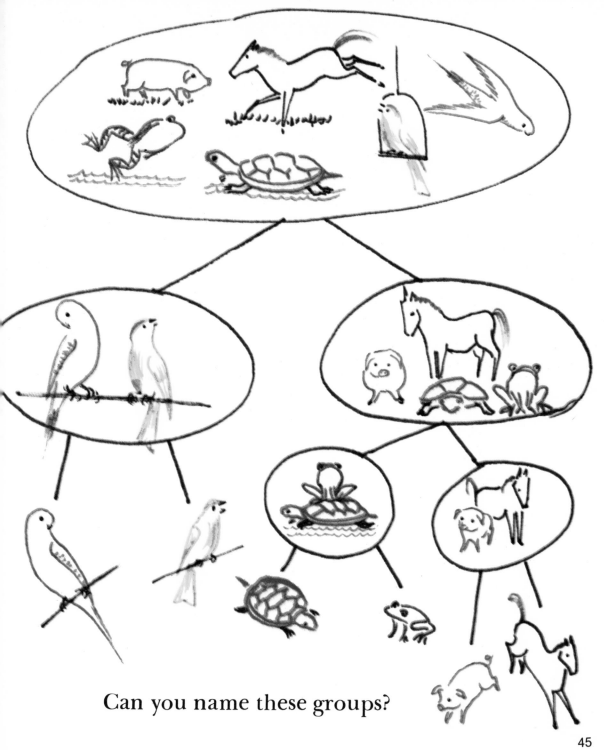

Can you name these groups?

Were your names the same as these?

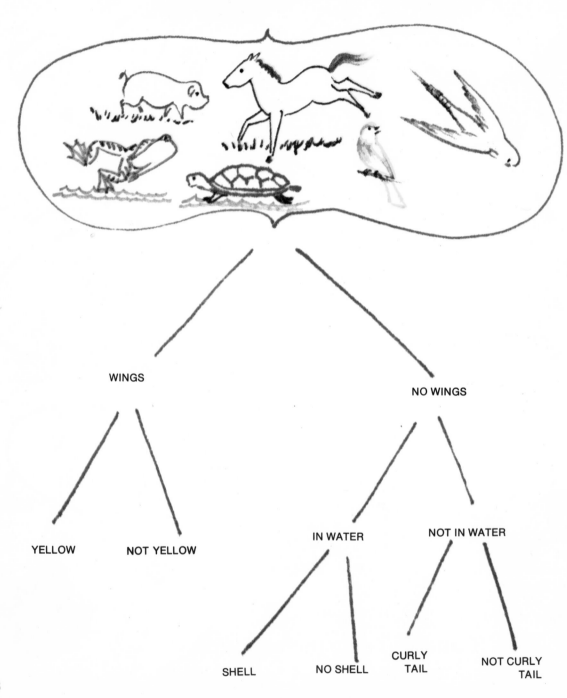

WINGS

NO WINGS

YELLOW

NOT YELLOW

IN WATER

NOT IN WATER

SHELL

NO SHELL

CURLY TAIL

NOT CURLY TAIL

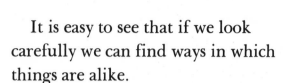

It is easy to see that if we look carefully we can find ways in which things are alike.

It is easy to see that if we look carefully we can find ways in which things are different.

Things may be alike or different in color.

They may be alike or different in shape.

They may be alike or different in size.

You are sure to find other ways in which things are alike and different.

Characteristics are used to classify things.

RENEWALS 691-4574

DATE DUE

SEP 2 1			
DEC 1 8			
APR 2 6			
NOV 11			
DEC 14			
MAY 1 0			
MAY 0 6			
APR 2 8			
MAY 0 7			
APR 1 2			
APR 2 7			

Demco, Inc. 38-293